Our Bodie

Our Bones

Charlotte Guillain

Raintree

www.raintreepublishers.co.uk

Visit our website to find out more information about Raintree books.

To order:

☎ Phone 0845 6044371

🖷 Fax +44 (0) 1865 312263

🖳 Email myorders@raintreepublishers.co.uk

Customers from outside the UK please telephone +44 1865 312262

Raintree is an imprint of Capstone Global Library Limited, a company incorporated in England and Wales having its registered office at 7 Pilgrim Street, London, EC4V 6LB – Registered company number: 6695582

Text © Capstone Global Library Limited 2010
First published in hardback in 2010
Paperback edition first published in 2011
The moral rights of the proprietor have been asserted.

Edited by Sian Smith, Laura Knowles, Nancy Dickmann, and Rebecca Rissman
Designed by Joanna Hinton-Malivoire
Original Illustrations © Capstone Global Library Ltd. 2010
Illustrated by Tony Wilson
Picture research by Ruth Blair and Mica Brancic
Production by Duncan Gilbert and Victoria Fitzgerald
Originated by Capstone Global Library Ltd
Printed and bound in China by South China Printing Company Ltd

ISBN 978 0 431 19510 0 (hardback)
14 13 12 11 10
10 9 8 7 6 5 4 3 2 1

ISBN 978 0 431 19520 9 (paperback)
15 14 13 12 11
10 9 8 7 6 5 4 3 2 1

British Library Cataloguing in Publication Data
Guillain, Charlotte.
 Our bones. -- (Acorn. Our bodies)
 1. Bones--Juvenile literature.
 I. Title II. Series
 612.7'5-dc22

Acknowledgements
We would like to thank the following for permission to reproduce photographs: Alamy pp.**4**, **22** (© JUPITERIMAGES/ BananaStock); © Capstone Global Library pp.**8**, **10** (Karon Dubke); Corbis pp.**11** (© Solus-Veer), **14** (© Morgan David de Lossy), **20** (© MM Productions); iStockphoto p.**16** (© Christopher Pattberg); Photolibrary pp.**13**, **5** (© Aflo Foto Agency), **15** (Onoky), **17**, **23** (© Phototake Science), **19** (© MedicImage Limited RF), **21** (© BSIP Medical); Science Photo Library p.**18** (PASIEKA); Shutterstock p.**9** (© Cindy Minear).

Front cover photograph of sisters doing cartwheels reproduced with permission of iStockphoto (©2008 Nancy Louie). Back cover photograph reproduced with permission of Photolibrary (Onoky/P Broze).

Every effort has been made to contact copyright holders of material reproduced in this book. Any omissions will be rectified in subsequent printings if notice is given to the publishers.

Contents

Body parts

Our bodies have many parts.

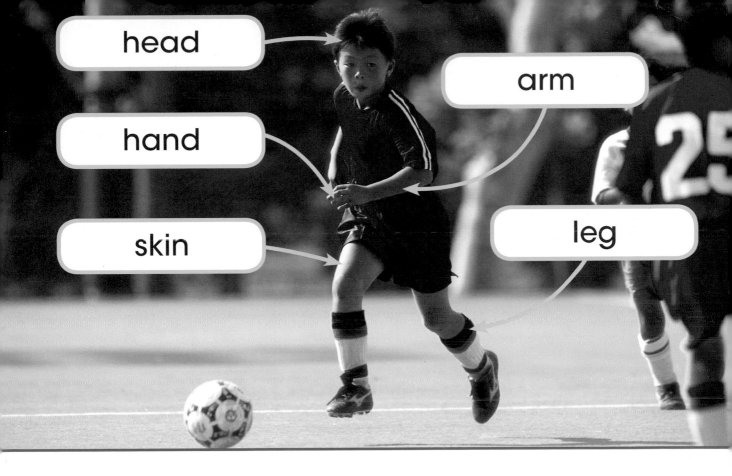

head

arm

hand

skin

leg

Our bodies have parts on
the outside.

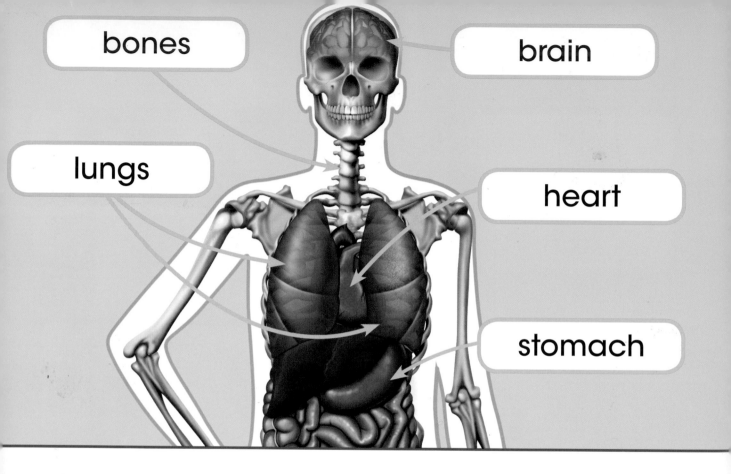

bones

brain

lungs

heart

stomach

Our bodies have parts on
the inside.

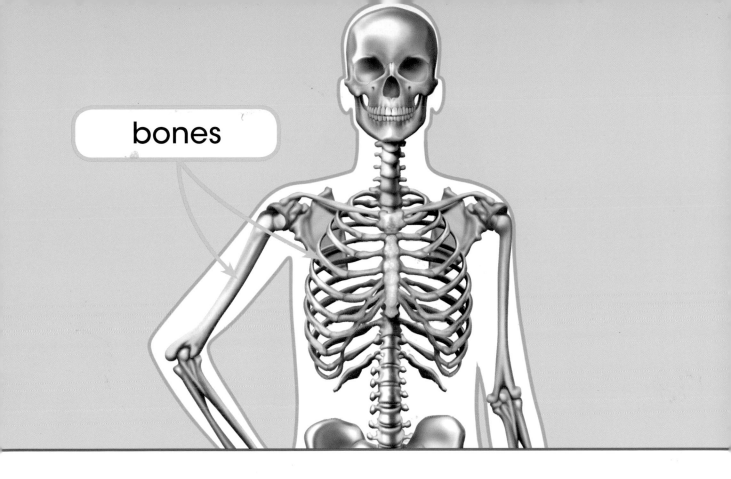

bones

Your bones are inside your body.

Your bones

You cannot see your bones.

Your bones are in all parts of
your body.

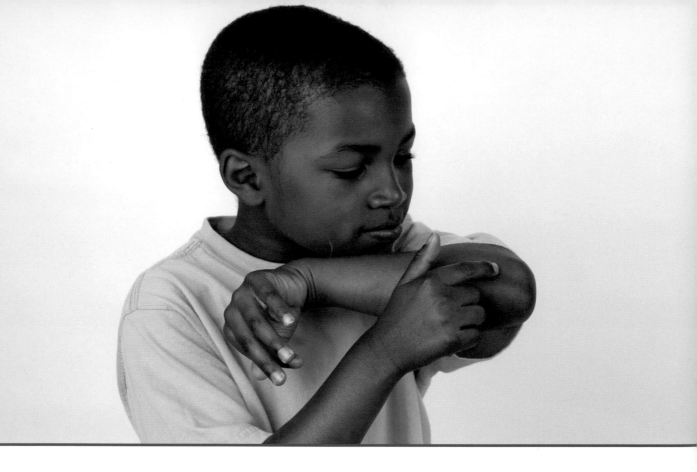

You can feel some of your bones.

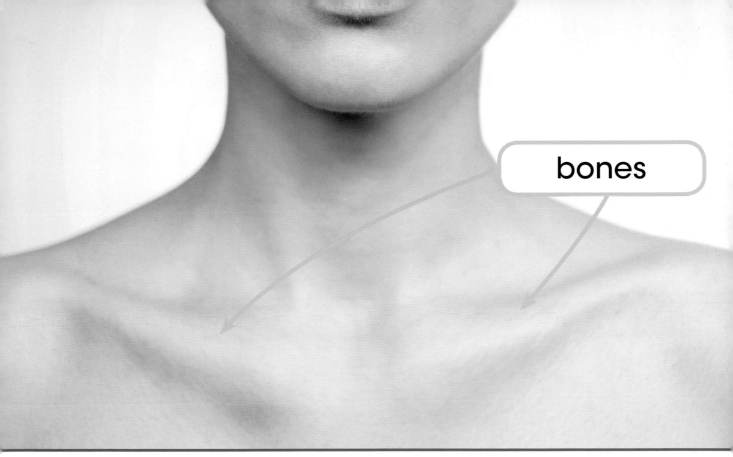

bones

You can see the shape of some bones.

Your skeleton

skeleton

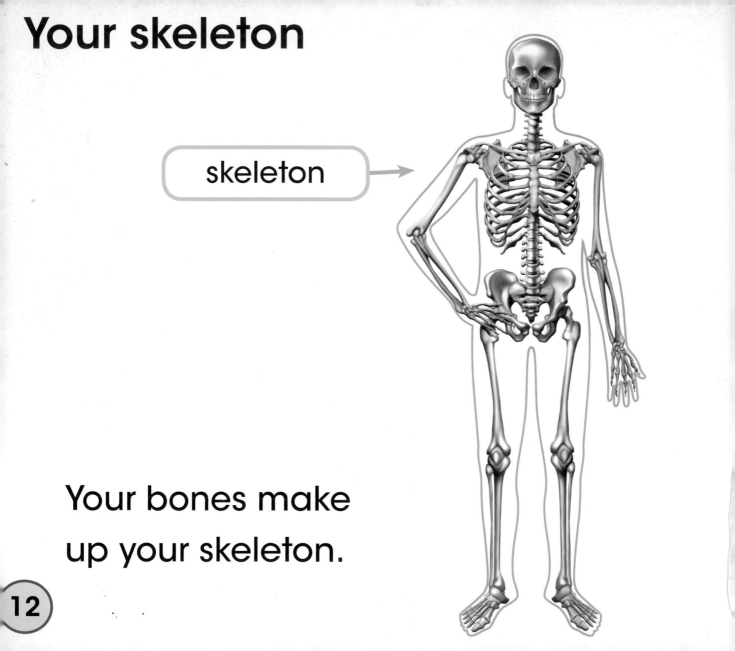

Your bones make up your skeleton.

Your skeleton holds your body up.

Your bones are hard and strong.

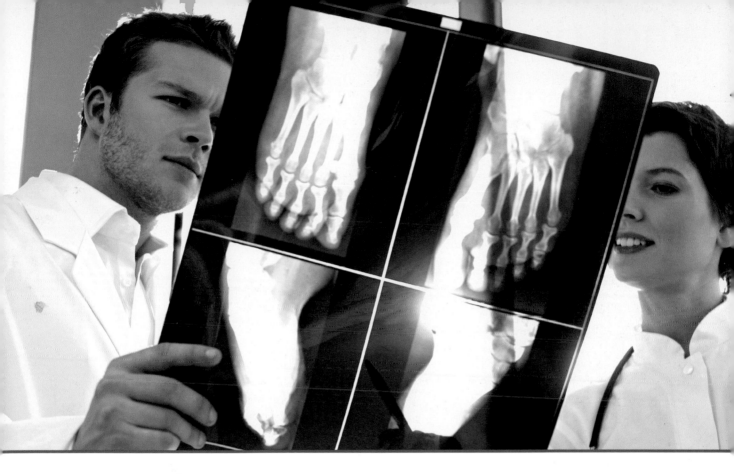

You can see your bones in an
X-ray photo.

What do bones look like?

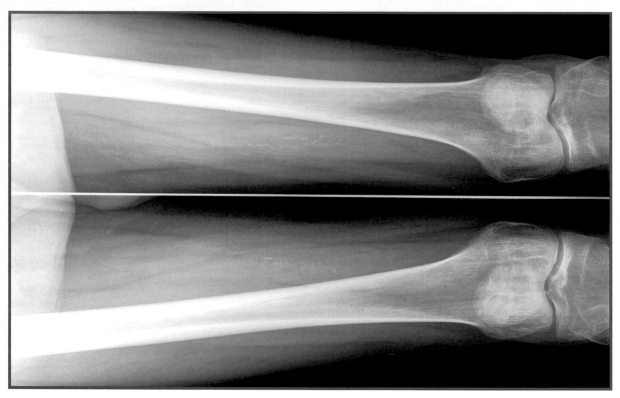

Some bones are long.

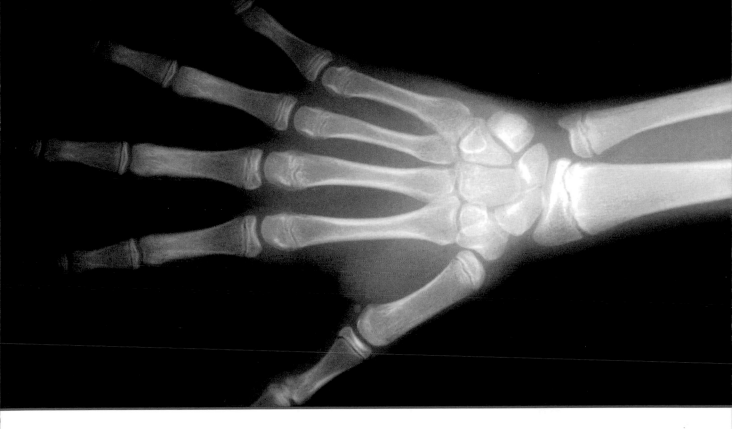

Some bones are small.

What do bones do?

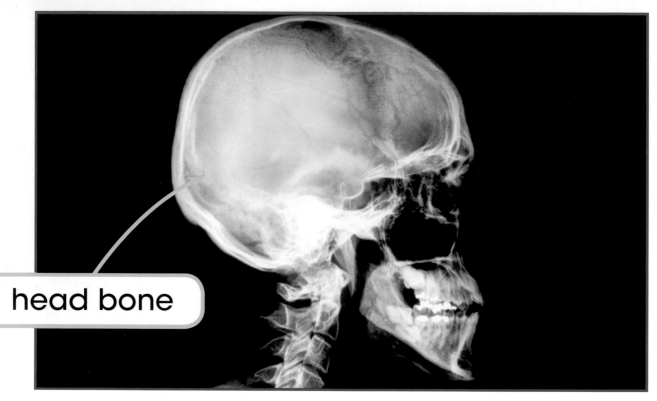

head bone

Bones in your head keep your brain safe.

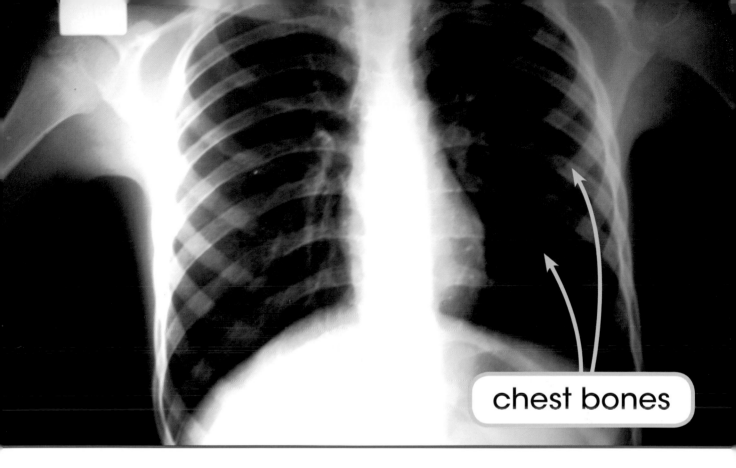

chest bones

Bones in your chest keep your lungs safe.

Staying healthy

You can exercise to help
your bones.

You can drink milk to help
your bones.

Where in your body are your bones?

Answer on page 24

Picture glossary

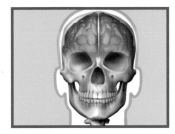 **brain** soft part of your body inside your head. You think with your brain.

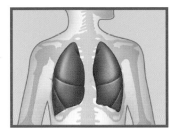 **lungs** two soft parts of your body inside your chest. You use your lungs when you breathe.

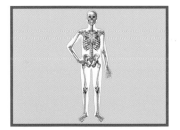 **skeleton** all the bones under your skin that hold your body up

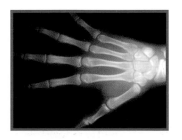 **X-ray** photograph that shows what the bones under your skin look like

Index

Answer to quiz on page 22:
Your bones are inside your body.

Notes to parents and teachers

Before reading

Ask the children to name the parts of their body they can see on the outside. Then ask them what parts of their body are inside. Make a list of them together and see if the children know what each body part does, for example, food goes into their stomachs. Discuss where their bones are and see if anyone knows what our bones do.

After reading

- Read *Funnybones* by Allan and Janet Ahlberg.
- Show the children a picture of a human skeleton. Ask them how many bones are in their arm. How many bones are in their leg? Look together at how bones can be different shapes and sizes. You could compare the human skeleton with pictures of different animal skeletons. How are they similar? How are they different?
- Ask the children if any of them have ever broken a bone. If anyone has, ask him or her to share with the class what happened at the hospital to fix the bone.